NATIONAL GEOGRAPHIC

RESCUED RIVERS

PIONEER EDITION

By Greta Gilbert

Contents

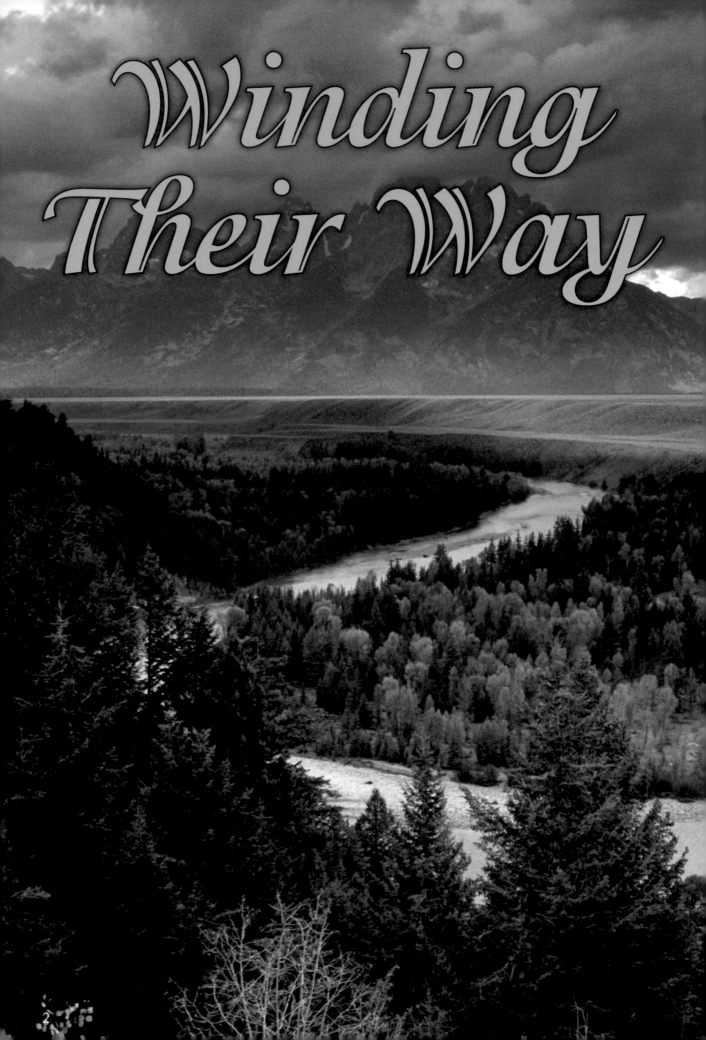

Winding Their Way

This is a story about rivers.
There are big rivers and
long rivers. There are lonely
rivers and strong rivers.
This is also a story about
plants, animals, and people.
These are the things that
depend on rivers.

You probably depend on a
river, too. That's because
most water in the United
States comes from lakes and rivers.
Rivers water crops. They cool
machines. They create energy. So
when you wash your hands or eat a
peach, it's probably thanks to a river.

The United States is lucky. Many
large rivers flow through the country.
So the country has a lot of fresh water.
There is a problem, however. In some
parts of the country, there is too much
water. Floods are common. In other
regions, there is often not enough
fresh water for people's needs.

To solve this problem, people
modify, or change, rivers. Some of the
changes to rivers are amazing. Other
changes are shocking. Read on to
follow the winding story of U.S. rivers.

By Greta Gilbert

Big River
MISSISSIPPI

In the 1800s, people thought the Mississippi River was wild. Why? It flooded the region without warning.

The floods were not all bad. They nourished, or fed, the land. Tiny bits of dirt and food, called **sediments**, floated in the water. They fed plants and tiny animals. The tiny animals grew and fed bigger animals. There was lots of life around the river.

The soils along the Mississippi were very rich. So crops grew easily. Farmers settled there. To make room for more farms, people cut down the forests around the river. They drained **wetlands**, too. And they built **levees**, or dirt mounds, to prevent floods.

The levees usually did their job. But as people removed wetlands, there were fewer places to absorb floodwaters. So floods became more serious.

In 1993, a massive flood hit. Water covered the land around the river. It swallowed towns. It did more damage than any other flood in U.S. history.

Today, people work to restore wetlands near the Mississippi. This helps prevent damage from floods. It will also help all the living things that depend on the river.

The Mississippi River flooded over its levees in 1993.

This is a dam on the Missouri River. It helps prevent floods.

Long River
MISSOURI

When Lewis and Clark explored the West, they followed the Missouri River. It is America's longest river.

The Missouri is another wild river. When the Missouri floods, dirt washes into the river. That's why it has the nickname "Muddy Mo."

The "mud" in the Missouri is sediment. The plants and animals living there need it to survive. One of those animals is the giant paddlefish. It has a mouth like a bucket and a nose like a beaver's tail.

There are feelers on the bottom of its nose. They help it find food in the murky water. Adult paddlefish are more than six feet long and weigh more than 200 pounds!

Today, paddlefish are in trouble. Why? One reason is dams. Over the years, people have built many large dams on the Missouri. Like levees, the dams help people. They control floods and store water. However, the dams cause river water to flow quickly. This washes away the calm, muddy water where paddlefish find their food.

Luckily, people want to save the paddlefish and its river habitat. The river habitat is being restored. This will help ensure a future for this amazing fish.

Paddlefish

5

Lonely River
COLORADO

One of the driest parts of the United States is the Desert Southwest. It includes the states of Colorado, Utah, Arizona, New Mexico, and Nevada.

In 1869, explorer John Wesley Powell came to a deep and isolated canyon. A river flowed through it. That canyon was the Grand Canyon. And the river was the Colorado.

Back then, the lonely line of the Colorado flowed to the sea without stopping. But Powell's trip showed that farmers would need a lot of land and water to live in the region. Crops would be hard to grow. Powell would be amazed if he returned there today.

Green fields bloom. Cities buzz. There are **reservoirs** and dams along most of the Colorado River.

The dams have brought water to the region. The desert is now farmland. However, there is still not enough water to meet everyone's needs. In some years, people take a lot of water out of the Colorado River. Then the river stops flowing before it reaches the sea.

People in the Desert Southwest are working hard to save the Colorado. They respect it and want to protect it.

This dam on the Colorado River creates Lake Powell.

Water rushes through this dam on the Columbia River.

WORDWISE

levee: an earth wall used to prevent flooding

reservoir: a lake that is used for storing water before people use it

sediment: bits of soil and plants deposited by river water

wetland: area that is often covered with water

Strong River
COLUMBIA

The Columbia is a powerful river. It whooshes down from the Canadian Rocky Mountains with incredible force. The Columbia is very steep. That is what makes it powerful.

That power does not stop one tough fish. The Columbia salmon is born in cold mountain streams. Then it swims thousands of miles to the ocean. At the end of its life, it swims back to where it was born—up the Columbia River. That's where it spawns, or reproduces.

In 1942, people finished building the Grand Coulee Dam on the river. They wanted the dam to turn the river's power into energy. It makes enough energy to power more than 2.3 million households! The dam is good for people but bad for salmon. Salmon can't get past the dam to spawn. So, the fish are in trouble.

Today, people are working hard to solve this problem. They build fish ladders that help salmon move past dams. They also spill water over the dams in the spring. This helps young salmon on their way to the sea.

A Yakima man fishes for salmon on the Columbia River.

Rivers Transformed

Levees and dams aren't the only way people change rivers. In California, people transform rivers completely.

Most of California's water is in the northern part of the state. But most of the people and farms are in the south.

People use special pumps and pipes to send water south from the Sacramento and San Joaquin Rivers. The water travels in concrete rivers.

These man-made rivers carry water to over 25 million people. The water also makes huge areas of farmland grow. These farms grow half of the country's fruits and vegetables.

Still, there is not enough water for everyone in California. So people look for ways to save the water they have.

The California Aqueduct carries water south.

The delta's water comes from the Sacramento and San Joaquin Rivers.

1 Steele's Mill Dam is in the center of this old photo.

2 Steele's Mill Dam is removed.

3 Steele's Mill Dam is gone now. And Hitchcock Creek runs freely today.

The Story Winds On

Today, people know that river ecosystems are important. They know that modifying, or changing, rivers can't solve all their water problems.

To protect rivers, people try to use less water. In Las Vegas, Nevada, people receive money to replace grass with native, water-conserving plants. In other cities, people use low-flow toilets and showerheads in their homes. Farmers use less water with "drip" watering systems. They plant crops that need less water, too.

Finally, people are restoring the wetlands of America. And thousands of kids participate in "Adopt-a-River" programs. They take part in river clean ups throughout the country.

You see, the story of U.S. rivers is not over. You get to write the next chapter. That's good news for the country. And it's good news for rivers.

People restore wetlands where the Mississippi River meets the Gulf of Mexico.

Restoring RIVERS

This is a fish ladder. It helps salmon move past a dam on the Columbia River. Then they can swim upstream to spawn.

People and businesses around Las Vegas replace grass with desert plants. They get money as a reward. They also save Colorado River water.

Many groups restore wetlands and woodlands along the Rio Grande. This helps native fish and birds that spend the winter in Texas.

WA

OR

Columbia River

NV

CA

Colorado River

AZ

Rio Grande River

NM

TX

People all around the United States are helping to restore rivers. Take a look at some of the their projects.

Bronx River

NY

People clean up trash along the Bronx River in New York. They keep track of the river's health, too. In 2007, a beaver made a home in the river. No one had seen a beaver there for 200 years!

Kissimmee River

FL

People began to restore wetlands around the Kissimmee River in 1999. Now many plants have returned. The number of birds has gone up, too.

Water for Life

Answer these questions to help keep rivers flowing!

1 Why are floods on the Mississippi River both good and bad?

2 How do dams on the Missouri River affect paddlefish?

3 Why doesn't the Colorado River flow all the way to the sea in some years?

4 What are the most important ideas about salmon in the article?

5 How do river restoration projects help protect plants and animals that depend on rivers?